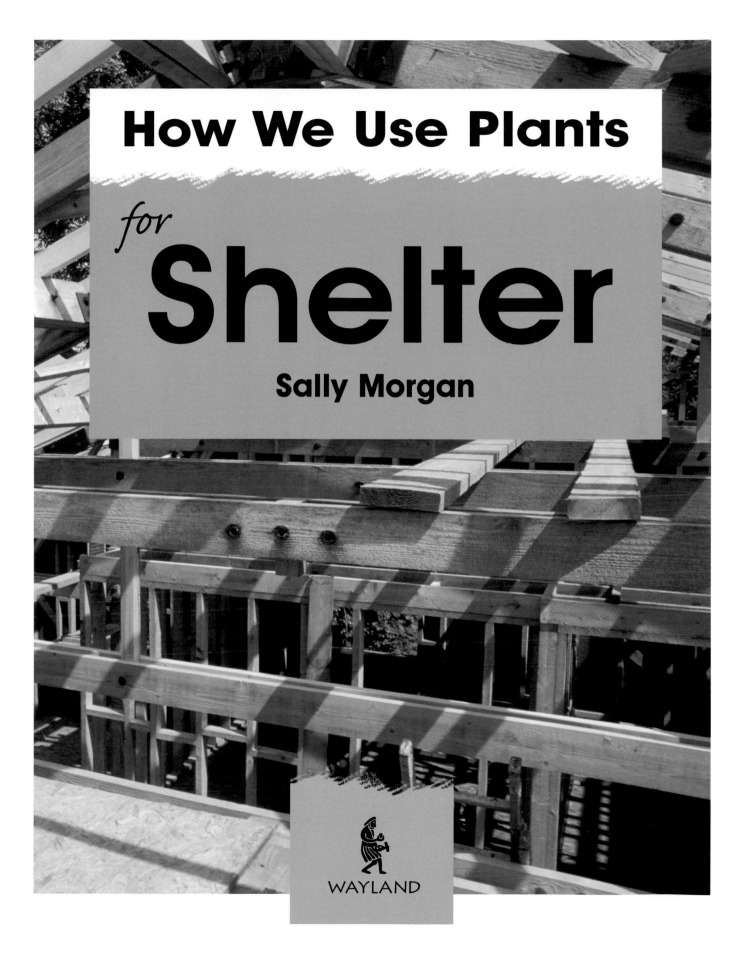

How We Use Plants

for Shelter

Sally Morgan

WAYLAND

First published in 2007 by Wayland

Copyright © Wayland 2007

Wayland
338 Euston Road
London NW1 3BH

Wayland Australia
Level 17/207 Kent Street
Sydney, NSW 2000

Editor: Camilla Lloyd
Designer: Matthew Lilly
Picture Researcher: Sally Morgan

Picture Acknowledgments: The author and publisher would
like to thank the following for allowing these pictures to be
reproduced in this publication. Cover: Ecoscene.
Ecoscene: 1, 4, 5, 6, 7, 10, 11, 12, 13, 14, 15, 16,
18, 19, 20, 21, 22, 23, 24, 25, 26, 27, 28;
Najlah Feanny/Corbis: 8; Justin Kase/Alamy
Images: 9; Philip Lewis/Alamy Images: 17;
Steve Atkins/Alamy Images: 27 (bottom right).

With special thanks to Ecoscene.

British Library Cataloguing in Publication Data:
Morgan, Sally
How we use plants for shelter
1. Plants, Useful - Juvenile literature 2. Building
materials - Juvenile literature
I. Title
581.6'36

ISBN: 978 0 7502 5064 1

Printed in China

Wayland is a division of Hachette Children's Books

Contents

Plants for shelter

Thousands of years ago, the first shelters made by people were made from plants. These shelters were very simple. The people used fallen tree **trunks** and branches to make a shelter like a **tent**. Then they covered their shelter with leaves to keep out the rain.

The roof of this house in Kenya is covered with palm leaves.

Today, modern homes use many types of building materials such as bricks, steel and concrete but plant materials are still important.

Wood is used to make doors, window frames, floors and the supports for the roof. In the tropical parts of the world, people use palms and bamboo for making their homes.

This cottage in the UK has a roof covered in reeds.

Plant materials should never run out so long as new trees, palms and other plants are planted to produce building materials for the future. The supplies of these materials are said to be **sustainable**.

Wood

Trees can be large plants. Each year, trees make new wood and their trunks get wider. Over time trees grow bigger and bigger.

This man is using a chain saw to cut down a large tree.

There are two main types of wood, **hardwood** and **softwood**. Hardwood comes from trees such as oak and beech. They are slow-growing trees with good quality wood. Softwood comes from fast-growing trees such as pine and spruce. It is cheaper than hardwood and there is more of it.

The trunks of trees are transported on large trucks to the timber mill.

Trees such as pine and spruce are planted in **plantations** as a **crop**. They are left to grow for 30 to 50 years and then cut down. The wood is taken to **timber** mills and cut into planks.

Woody materials

Wood can be made into a range of wood products. Plywood is made from three or more thin layers of wood which are glued together. This makes the sheets of plywood strong. Plywood is a cheap material as it can be made from poor quality wood. It is used on floors and for making furniture and cupboards.

Have A Go!

• Have a look around your home and see if you can find examples of plywood and chipboard. What were they used for? Can you find any veneers?

Tree trunks can be sawn into planks and used to make things.

Another cheap material is chipboard. It is made from wood chips glued together to form sheets. MDF stands for Medium Density Fibreboard. It is like chipboard and it is made from fibres of birch and larch glued together.

A veneer is a thin sheet of wood that can be stuck onto a poorer quality wood or chipboard to make it look like good quality wood.

The roof of this house is supported by wooden beams. The floor of the loft is made of MDF.

Timber homes

When Europeans first arrived in North America, they made simple log cabins from wood. Trees were **felled** and the trunks were used to make the walls.

Many older houses dating back from Tudor and Elizabethan times have timber frames. The wood can be seen from the outside on this house.

Larger structures such as houses and barns can be built using a timber frame. In a timber-framed building, long lengths of wood form the framework and they support the whole house. The lengths of wood are held together with wooden pegs.

Did You Know?

The wood used in timber frames is often called green wood because it is freshly cut and it has not dried out. It gradually shrinks over time.

This carpenter is building the timber frame of a new house.

The walls are formed by filling the spaces in the timber frame with brick or smaller lengths of wood. Sloping pieces of timber are used to build the roof. Then tiles, slates or **thatch** are laid on these roof supports to keep water out.

11

Thatching

For thousands of years, people have used reeds and **straw** as roofing materials. A roof made of plant material is called a thatched roof. Plants were chosen to put on the roof because they were light in weight. The buildings of the time were not strong enough to support the weight of anything heavier.

Did You Know?

The first Globe Theatre in London was built in 1599. It burnt down fourteen years later because a spark from a canon used on the stage landed on the thatched roof and started a fire.

Reeds are cut and bundled together ready to be used on a roof.

Many types of plants can be used as thatch. Palm leaves are used in tropical countries. In Europe, reeds, straw, willow and grasses are used.

Thatched roofs are common on the island of Madiera, which lies in the Atlantic Ocean.

The plants are harvested and made into small bundles. The bundles are laid on the roof and secured in place with twigs. A second layer is added to make sure the roof keeps out water. The thatcher can carve interesting shapes into the roof.

The walls and roof of this Sri Lankan family's house are made from palm leaves.

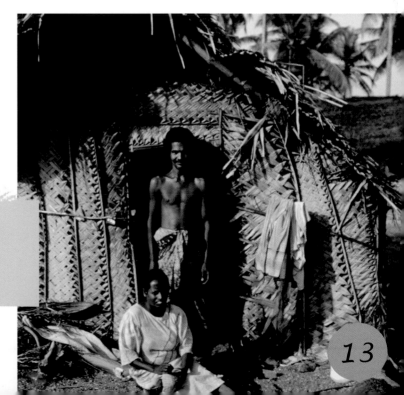

Straw homes

Straw is the dry **stalk** of a cereal plant, such as wheat and barley, that is left behind after the seeds have been harvested. Most straw is used as animal bedding but it can be used as a building material too.

Straw is left on the field by the combine harvester after the seeds of the cereal have been collected.

Houses can be made from straw bales instead of bricks. Straw bales are good at keeping out the rain and cold and keeping the heat inside the house. They are strong but lightweight.

Beams of wood or steel stop the bales moving. The outermost bales are covered with mesh to keep rats, mice and birds from nesting in the straw!

Straw is allowed to dry and then bundled into bales. The bales are stored in a dry place until they are needed.

The walls of this new house are made from straw bales on a wooden frame. Holes are cut to make windows and doors.

Tents

Tents are temporary shelters that protect people from wind, rain and the cold. **Nomadic** people move from place to place, often following their herds of grazing animals. They use tents because they can be put up and taken down easily.

These weavers in the Himalayan Mountains are working in a tent made from plant materials.

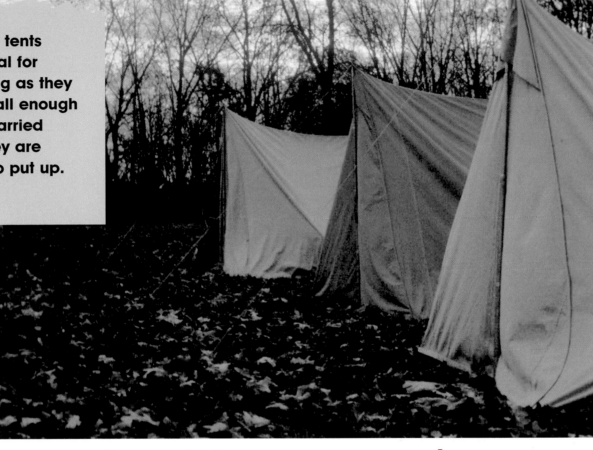

Canvas tents are ideal for camping as they are small enough to be carried and they are quick to put up.

Tents range in size. The smallest ones are for one or two people, but the largest are the size of many rooms. Tents can be supported by a central wooden pole, a series of hoops or by several upright poles.

Once the frame is in place, material is laid over the frame and secured in place so that it does not blow away. Often this material is a **canvas** made from the cotton, jute or hemp plant.

Did You Know?

One of the largest tents in the world was the Grand Marquee at the Chelsea Flower Show in London. It was used during the 1990s and covered 1.4 hectares and weighed 65 tonnes.

Bamboo for building

Bamboo is an important building material especially in Asia. It is used in the same way as wood. Bamboo is a fast-growing grass. Each year the canes or **stems** are harvested and new ones grow back the following year.

The scaffolding used on this building in China is made from bamboo.

The largest bamboo canes are used to make the frame of a house and even to support the roof. Bamboo canes can also be used as **scaffolding**, in the same way that steel is used.

Some of the longest bamboo canes are 3 metres long and reach a diameter (width) of 12 centimetres.

Bamboo canes are made into boards that can be used to make walls and floor coverings. The canes are split up the middle and woven together. Glue is spread on one side to harden the whole structure so that it forms a stiff board.

It's A Question!

Bamboo canes are hollow. Can you think of any uses for hollow canes?

Paints

A paint has three main ingredients. It contains a **pigment** that gives the colour, a **binder** that sticks the pigment to the object being painted and a **solvent** that holds the pigment and binder together. Without a solvent, the pigment and binder would form two separate layers in the paint.

Paints are used to add colour to walls, wood and other surfaces. Paints can protect wood too. Wood that is left out in the rain will eventually rot and have to be replaced. Paint keeps most of the water out, so the wood lasts longer.

In watercolour paints, the solvent is gum arabic, something that comes from acacia trees.

All these ingredients can come from plants, although many modern paints use **artificial** ingredients. Binders can be made from gum or plant sap. A natural solvent is linseed oil. It can also be made from the peel of citrus fruits.

It's A Question!

Decorators use two types of paint, one is called gloss paint and the other is emulsion paint. Can you find out which type of paint would be used to paint over wood?

Unused paints should be taken to special sites like this one in North Wales. Then it can be disposed of safely or sent to be recycled.

Plant pigments

Many different pigments can be found in plants. For example, you may get a green stain on pale coloured clothes if you sit on grass.

The stains from orange and blackcurrant drinks are really difficult to get out of clothes. This is because the pigment sticks to the cloth and cannot be removed.

These herbs and spices contain different coloured pigments.
1. Dill
2. Coriander
3. Paprika
4. Turmeric
5. Cinammon
6. Nutmeg
7. Cumin
8. Chives
9. Rosemary

Some of the oldest plant pigments in use include saffron, turmeric and carrots. However, there are many other pigments. Common examples include walnut, blueberry, beetroot, paprika and hibiscus flowers.

Have A Go!

● It is easy to see how plant pigment can be used to colour something. You need a piece of white cotton and some chopped beetroot. Place the beetroot in a pan of water and simmer gently. Add the cotton and leave for about 5 minutes. Remove it using a wooden spoon and leave it to dry. You will need an adult to help you.. It should now be purple from the beetroot.

A purple-red pigment is obtained from the hibiscus flower.

1

6

9

Plants for walls and floors

A number of plant materials are used in the home. Curtains are made from cotton and chairs are made from rattan. Paper wallpaper made from trees can cover the walls.

In some new homes, the **insulation** in the walls is made from recycled paper. Paper insulation is full of air spaces and this traps the heat inside the home so that little escapes.

The insulation in this new home comes from old newspapers that have been broken up to form a paste. Paper is made from trees.

Floors may be covered by floorboards made of wood. Carpets are laid over the floorboards. Although many carpets are made from wool, plant fibres such as sisal, sea grass and hemp can be used too. These carpets are very hard-wearing.

This man is making a woven mat from large palm leaves.

Have A Go!

• Is the doormat at the entrance to your home made from plant fibres? Have a look. Mats made from sisal or coconut fibres are very rough so that they trap the dirt from the bottom of shoes.

How the oak tree is used

Oak trees have been used as a source of high quality timber for thousands of years. An oak tree can grow to a great size and the timber is ideal for building ships and homes as well as many other things.

Timber:
Oak wood is a long-lasting hardwood. It is used to make timber-framed buildings, furniture, doors and windows.

Charcoal:
The smaller branches from an oak tree are not suitable for timber but can be made into **charcoal**. Charcoal is used as a source of heat on a fire or barbecue.

Acorns:
The fruit of the oak tree is called an acorn. Acorns are eaten by many animals such as squirrels and pigs.

Furniture:
Furniture such as beds, tables and chairs are often made from oak. The oak can be stained to give a light or dark colour to the wood.

Build your own model hut!

Have a look at the photo on this page. This is the first stage in the building of a traditional stilted hut in Zambia. See if you can build a model of this at home using plant materials. You will need a piece of cardboard about 20 x 15 cm, some twigs, dried grass or leaves, glue and some string.

Step 1

The piece of cardboard forms the floor of the hut. Make a small hole near each of the four corners. Take four twigs that are about 20 cm long and push one through each of the holes. Each twig needs to stick out about 5 cm below the cardboard.

Step 2

Make two holes along each side and push through some more twigs. Now your model is at the same stage as the hut in the photo.

Step 3

Your next job is to thread some long twigs horizontally through the top of the vertical twigs and secure with string. These twigs form the top of the four 'walls' of the hut. You can weave some dried grass or twigs between the uprights to form a woven wall.

Step 4

The roof can be made from twigs attached at an angle to the top of the wall. You will need quite a few roof supports to attach the thatch securely with glue.

Step 5

The thatch can be made from dried grass or leaves and tied with string. Cut out some doors and windows. You can make the doors from wood or from a woven rectangle of grass.

Glossary

artificial not natural, made by people.

binder the part of paint that makes it stick to the object being painted.

canvas a rough cloth used to make sails and tents.

charcoal the black coals formed by burning wood slowly. Charcoal can be used to heat things on a barbecue.

crop a plant grown by people for a special use.

felled cut down.

hardwood wood that comes from slow-growing trees.

insulation something that prevents heat escaping.

nomadic nomads are wandering people, nomadic is a characteristic of wandering people.

pigment a substance that gives colour to paint.

plantation an area of land where crops or trees are planted.

scaffolding a series of poles and platforms put up around a building so that workmen can reach the higher parts of the building.

softwood wood that comes from fast-growing trees.

solvent the part in paint that holds the pigment and the binder together.

stalk stem of a plant.

stem part of a plant that supports the leaves.

straw the dried stalk of a cereal plant.

sustainable a way of managing a resource, like wood from trees so that there is enough for the future.

tent temporary shelters made from material like canvas supported by poles.

thatch plant materials used to make the roof of a house.

timber wood from trees that is mostly used for building materials.

trunk the name given to the stem of a tree.

wood a substance made by trees that makes up much of the tree trunk.

Further information

Books

Plants and Us
by Angela Royston,
Heinemann, 1999

Plants and People
by Sally Morgan,
Belitha Press, 2002

Roots, Stems and Leaves
by Sally Morgan,
Belitha Press, 2002

Websites

The Great Plant Escape
*http://www.urbanext.uiuc.edu/gpe
/index.html*
A fun website where you can be a
detective and find out more
about plants.

**In Search of the Ways of
Knowing Trail**
*http://www.brookfieldzoo.org/pagegen
/wok/ways_index.html*
Interactive games in which you can
explore the plants of the rainforest and
discover how they are used.

Answers

P18 pipes

P21 gloss paint is an oil-based
paint and is used on wood.
Emulsion paint is used on walls.

Index